PAUL REVERE'S RIDE

A FLY on the WALL HISTORY

Medford

Charlestown

Boston

Lexington

Concord

Charles River

N
W E
S

BY THOMAS KINGSLEY TROUPE   ILLUSTRATED BY JOMIKE TEJIDO

PICTURE WINDOW BOOKS

Hi, I'm Maggie, and this is my brother, Horace.

We've been "flies on the wall" during important events in history.

We saw cavemen make the first fire.

We watched the *Titanic* set sail across the ocean.

We even walked on the moon (inside space suits, naturally).

But one of our most thrilling adventures was riding with Paul Revere at the start of the American Revolution ...

2

We were buzzing around the American Colonies in 1775. The colonies were 13 lands ruled by Great Britain. One day those lands would become the United States of America. But for now the British controlled them, and many colonists were angry.

Why was there so much anger? Well, the British made the colonists pay taxes. Lots of them. But the colonists were given no say in the British government. They were expected to pay taxes like British citizens, but they didn't have all the rights British citizens had. Many people felt it wasn't fair. Everyone was afraid fighting would break out.

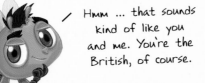

So the colonists don't like the British bossing them around.

Hmm ... that sounds kind of like you and me. You're the British, of course.

Ha, ha, very funny, Horace.

Horace and I found a silversmith shop owned by Paul Revere. He made teapots and other shiny things. While Horace was goofing around, Paul looked out the window. He mumbled something about the British—and it wasn't good. He also mumbled something about making a plan.

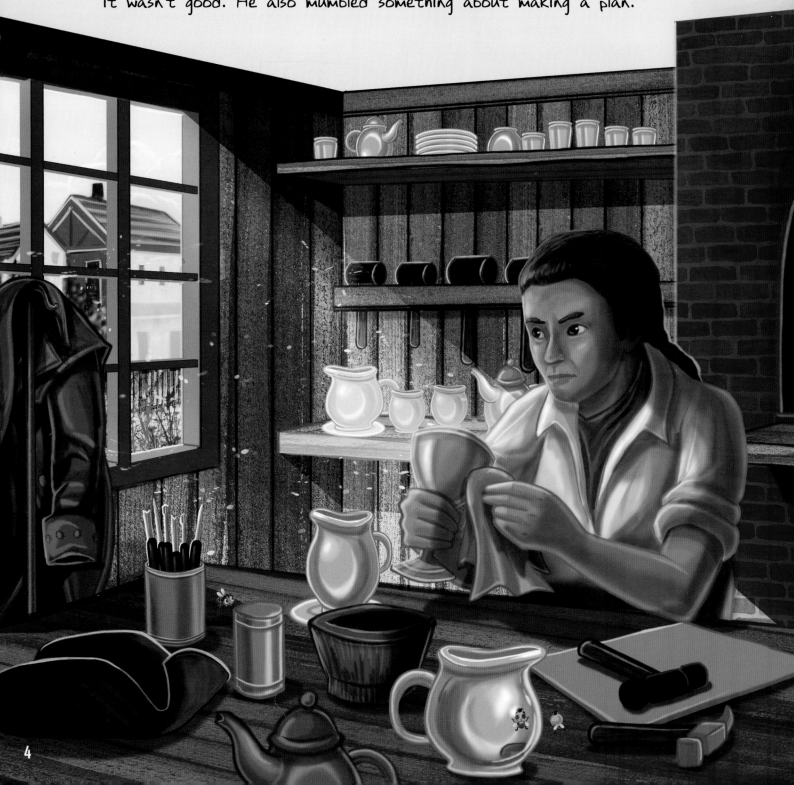

Paul told his wife he was riding to the nearby town of Lexington. He needed to talk with Hancock and Adams right away.

So who are Hancock and Adams?

Should I know those guys?

John Hancock and Samuel Adams are rebels, or revolutionaries.

Later they'll be called patriots.

They believe the British shouldn't control the colonies.

★ ★ ★

Many American rebels belonged to a secret group called the Sons of Liberty. They wanted to stop unfair treatment by the British government.

★ ★ ★

Horace and I wanted to see these rebels for ourselves. We hitched a ride with Paul to Lexington. (I LOVE the smell of horses!) We rode past Regulars patrolling the streets.

* * *

The colonists called British soldiers "Regulars."

* * *

In Lexington, Paul talked with Hancock and Adams. They thought the British might find their hidden ammunition and flour in Concord. After they finished talking, word was sent to Concord. The rebels needed to hide their supplies before the Regulars found them.

Who cares if the Regulars find their flower?

Flowers are way too stinky for me. I prefer the smell of dead fish, thank you.

They mean flour. F-L-O-U-R. The stuff humans use to bake things.

Oh. Makes sense. They don't want the colonists to have bullets ... OR food to eat!

Before Paul returned home, he stopped in Charlestown. He and another rebel named Colonel Conant discussed their plan. They would warn people when the Regulars were coming by hanging lanterns. And they'd hang them from the tallest building in Boston—the North Church.

One light meant the Regulars were marching. Two lights meant they were taking boats. "One if by land, two if by sea." The colonel said he'd be on the lookout.

They need lights? My firefly buddies could help.

The lights need to be bright and up high so everyone can see.

I don't think firefly butts get that bright!

* * *

The North Church's steeple was the tallest in Boston at the time. It stood 191 feet (58 meters) tall.

* * *

A few days later, a rebel leader named Dr. Joseph Warren told Paul the British Navy had put their boats in the water. They were on the move!

Paul needed to ride to Lexington and warn Hancock and Adams. But first he needed to stop at Robert Newman's house. Newman was the sexton at the North Church. Paul waited near a window, while Horace bounced against the glass. I peeked inside. There were REGULARS in there!

* * *

A sexton is a caretaker for a church.

* * *

Weird. Why are the British soldiers at Robert Newman's house?

It looks like they are renting rooms there. Lots of British soldiers do that.

Seems IRREGULAR, doesn't it?

As soon as the Regulars started playing cards, Newman went to his
bedroom. He snuck out the window so the soldiers wouldn't see him.
Paul said it was time for the signal. Newman ran to the North Church.
Two friends of his were already waiting there.

Newman and one of his friends climbed to the top of the steeple. (While they climbed, Horace flew.) There they lit two lanterns. They aimed them toward Charlestown. After no more than a minute, the men took down the lights. I hoped everyone got the message.

While the signals were being hung, Paul and I snuck toward the Charles River. We avoided the soldiers walking in the streets. Paul told his dog he needed to warn anyone who hadn't seen the lights.

What was it like up there in the steeple, Horace?

Kind of scary. You know I'm afraid of heights. But I did meet a nice moth named Barry.

* * *

There's a folktale that says Paul forgot his spurs. He wrote a note to his wife and pinned it to his dog's collar. He sent the dog home and waited. The dog returned a few minutes later with Paul's spurs in his mouth. This story probably isn't true, but it's still a good one!

* * *

Horace quickly joined Paul and me at the Charles River. Horace loves boats. I don't. The waves were really knocking us around, and I was feeling sick. But Paul's friends kept us afloat. We snuck right past a big ship Paul called the *Somerset*. He said it was British.

* * *

Some stories say that to make the oars quieter, Paul's friend borrowed a woman's petticoat. He and Paul wrapped the cloth around the oarlocks to muffle the sound.

I was so happy to be out of the rowboat. Horace and I followed Paul into Charlestown. He stopped to talk to Colonel Conant. The colonel and some Minutemen said they saw the signal and were getting ready. They also warned Paul that there were already Regulars in town.

A man brought a big horse over for Paul to ride. He told Paul her name was Brown Beauty. She WAS a beauty, and she smelled great!

It's getting late. Isn't it bedtime?

It's close to 11 p.m. We have to get to Lexington and warn everyone along the way.

It's going to be a long night!

★ ★ ★

The Minutemen were a small group of colonial soldiers. They were called Minutemen because they could be ready for battle in a minute's time.

★ ★ ★

We were off! We spotted Regulars by a tree, and they rode after us. Brown Beauty ran like the wind through Charlestown Neck.

We raced down Medford Road, and one of the riders tried to cut us off. His horse galloped into a clay pond and got stuck. Paul kicked his spurs, and we raced out of town.

Wow, those Regulars look angry, don't they, Maggie?

Sure do! Their faces are as red as their coats!

★ ★ ★

The town of Lexington was 12 miles (19 kilometers) from Charlestown.

We finally arrived in Lexington around midnight. Paul patted Brown Beauty, and we headed toward a large house. One of the guards outside stopped us. He told Paul to keep the noise down. The people inside were sleeping.

"Noise? You'll have noise enough before long! The Regulars are coming out!" Paul yelled.

Hancock came to the window, dressed in his pajamas.
"Come in, Revere," he said. "Tell us your news."

Paul told everyone inside that the Regulars were on their way. Another man showed up about a half hour later. His name was William Dawes. He said he rode out of Boston before the soldiers stopped anyone else from leaving. Dawes delivered the same message.

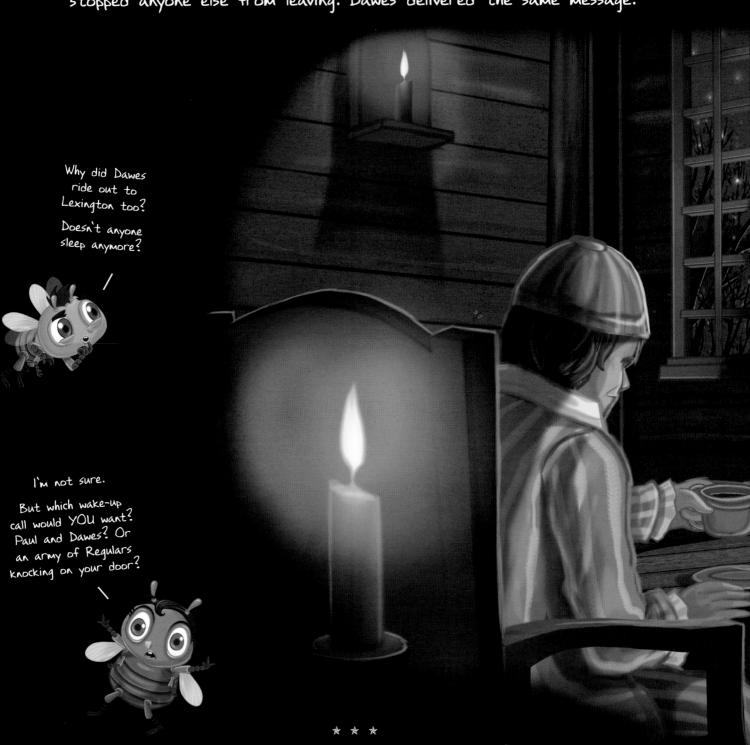

Why did Dawes ride out to Lexington too?

Doesn't anyone sleep anymore?

I'm not sure.

But which wake-up call would YOU want? Paul and Dawes? Or an army of Regulars knocking on your door?

⭐ ⭐ ⭐

William Dawes was another member of the Sons of Liberty.
Dr. Warren sent him as a backup to Lexington, in case Paul didn't make it.

⭐ ⭐ ⭐

Hancock and Adams said they'd be safe. They also told Paul and Dawes they needed to ride to Concord. The people there needed to hide the ammunition.

Brown Beauty galloped like her hooves were on fire. We stopped at every house we saw along the way. Paul knocked on doors and called out until people came outside.

"The Regulars are out!" Paul told them.

Some of the Minutemen grabbed their rifles. A Son of Liberty named Dr. Samuel Prescott offered to ride with us. He wanted to help warn more people.

* * *

Paul Revere didn't shout, "The British are coming!" as many once believed.
This would have confused everyone, since the colonists *were* British.

* * *

Halfway to Concord, we ran into trouble. There were Regulars everywhere! We tried to run away, but Brown Beauty was tired. Dawes' horse was scared and threw him off. Dr. Prescott was the only one who escaped.

Whoa!

Did you see the doctor's horse jump that fence?

Awesome!

I did! It was like the horse had spring-loaded hooves!

I just hope Dr. Prescott gets to Concord in time.

Those sneaky Regulars are EVERYWHERE ... like bugs!

The Regulars asked Paul a lot of questions. Paul told them he had warned the entire countryside. The colonists were ready to fight!

The Regulars took Brown Beauty and then let us go. Paul had to walk back to Lexington on foot as the war began.

Shortly after Paul Revere was let go, 700 Regulars marched into Lexington. A group of about 75 colonists was ready for them, thanks to Paul Revere, William Dawes, and Dr. Samuel Prescott. No one knows who fired the first shot, but it was known as the "shot heard around the world." Eight colonists were killed in the battle, and 10 more were wounded.

The Regulars marched to Concord to destroy the ammunition. On a bridge just outside Concord, they saw the colonists had cannons and even more weapons. Dozens more men died in the fighting, but the British turned back to Boston. The colonists had won their first battle of the Revolutionary War.

TIMELINE

1765 ✶ PASSAGE OF THE STAMP ACT
This law from the British government makes all American colonists pay a tax on every piece of printed paper.

MARCH 5, 1770 ✶ BOSTON MASSACR
A crowd of angry colonists and a few British get into an argument on the streets of Bost British fire guns into the crowd, killing three Two more colonists die later from their wou

1774 ✶ PASSAGE OF THE INTOLERABLE ACTS
The British government issues four new laws for the colonists. The first law closes Boston Harbor. The British want to be paid back for the tea the colonists ruined during the Boston Tea Party. The second law gives the royal governor, General Thomas Gage, complete control over the colony. The third law protects British officers who enforce the law. It lets them go to England or another colony to stand trial. The fourth law lets British soldiers live in empty buildings throughout the colonies.

DECEMBER 16, 1773 ✶ BOSTON TEA PARTY
Angry about British taxes on tea, Sam Adams and the Sons of Liberty take a stand. Some members of the Sons board three British ships in Boston Harbor. Together they throw 342 chests of tea overboard.

SEPTEMBER 5, 1774 ✶ FIRST CONTINENTAL CONGRESS
A meeting of delegates from 12 of the 13 colonies is held in Philadelphia to respond to the Intolerable Acts. The meeting lasts from September 5 to October 26, 1774.

JULY 4, 1776 ✶ DECLARATION OF INDEPENDENCE
Thomas Jefferson writes a historic document that explains why the colonies should no longer be ruled by the British government.

APRIL 19, 1775 ✶ BATTLES OF LEXINGTON AND CONCORD
The first battles of the American Revolutionary War take place.

SEPTEMBER 19 THROUGH OCTOBER 7, 1
BATTLES OF SARATOGA
A series of American victories convinces the Fren colonists and fight for America. The French prov and fight the British on land and sea.

OCTOBER 19, 1781 ✶ SURRENDER OF YORKTOWN
The British send 8,000 troops to Yorktown and expect more from sea. However, the French navy keeps British ships from reaching Yorktown. With an army of 17,000, George Washington and French general Jean-Baptiste Rochambeau move to Yorktown and surround the town. They block supplies from reaching the British soldiers. Without food and ammunition, the British cannot continue to fight. They give up.

SEPTEMBER 3, 1783 ✶ TREATY OF PARIS IS SIGNED
This document serves as an agreement to end the Revolutionary War and to recognize the United States of America

GLOSSARY

ammunition–bullets and other objects that can be fired from weapons

colony–an area that has been settled by people from another country; a colony is ruled by another country

Minutemen–a small, select group of American colonists who were ready and willing to fight at a moment's notice

petticoat–a piece of clothing worn under a skirt; often made with a ruffled, pleated, or lace edge

rebel–someone who fights against a government or the people in charge of something

Regular–the American colonists' name for a British solider

revolution–a violent uprising by the people of a country that changes its system of government

sexton–a caretaker for a church

silversmith–a person who makes items out of silver, such as spoons, jewelry, and teapots

Sons of Liberty–a secret group of American colonists who fought against British taxes and eventually pushed for the colonies' independence from Great Britain

spur–a small, metal wheel worn on the back of a boot

steeple–a tall tower atop a church

tax–money that people or businesses must give to the government to pay for what the government does

THINK ABOUT IT

1. Explain how lanterns spread the news of the approaching British soldiers. Include what the number of lanterns meant and why they were hung in the tower of Boston's North Church. (Key Ideas and Details)

2. Minutemen were a small, select group of young men who fought for the American Colonies. Why were they called Minutemen? How could they be more useful than a regular army? (Integration of Knowledge and Ideas)

3. Paul Revere rode Brown Beauty across the countryside to warn that the Regulars were coming. How might news like that spread today? (Integration of Knowledge and Ideas)

READ MORE

Goddu, Krystyna Poray. *What's Your Story, Paul Revere?* Cub Reporter Meets Famous Americans. Minneapolis: Lerner Publications, 2016.

Min, Ellen. *The Midnight Ride of Paul Revere: One If by Land, Two If by Sea.* Spotlight on American History. New York: PowerKids Press, 2016.

Scarbrough, Mary Hertz. *Heroes of the American Revolution.* The Story of the American Revolution. North Mankato, Minn.: Capstone Press, 2013.

INTERNET SITES

FactHound offers a safe, fun way to find Internet sites related to this book.
All of the sites on FactHound have been researched by our staff.

Here's all you do:
Visit *www.facthound.com*
Type in this code: 9781479597857

Check out projects, games and lots more at
www.capstonekids.com

INDEX

Look for all the books in the series:

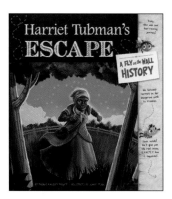   

Special thanks to our adviser, Kevin Byrne, PhD, Professor Emeritus of History, Gustavus Adolphus College, for his expertise.

Picture Window Books is published by Capstone,
1710 Roe Crest Drive, North Mankato, Minnesota 56003
www.mycapstone.com

Library of Congress Cataloging-in-Publication Data
Names: Troupe, Thomas Kingsley, author. | Tejido, Jomike, illustrator
Title: Paul Revere's ride : a fly on the wall history / by Thomas Kingsley Troupe.
Description: North Mankato, Minnesota : Capstone Press, [2017] | Series: Nonfiction picture books. Fly on the wall history | Includes bibliographical references and index. | Audience: Grades K–3.
Identifiers: LCCN 2016034451 | ISBN 9781479597857 (library binding) | ISBN 9781479597895 (paperback) | ISBN 9781479597932 (eBook : .pdf)
Subjects: LCSH: Revere, Paul, 1735–1818–Juvenile literature. | Statesmen–Massachusetts–Biography–Juvenile literature. | Massachusetts–Biography–Juvenile literature. | Massachusetts–History–Revolution, 1775–1783–Juvenile literature.
Classification: LCC F69.R43 T76 2017 | DDC 973.3/311092 [B]–dc23
LC record available at https://lccn.loc.gov/2016034451

Editor: Jill Kalz
Designer: Sarah Bennett
Creative Director: Nathan Gassman
Production Specialist: Steve Walker

The illustrations in this book were planned with pencil on paper and finished with digital paints.

Printed and bound in the USA
010059S17CG